All That Thrills My Soul

Hymns of Faith & Devotion for Solo Piano

Arranged by

LAVAWAN RILEY

Lillenas PUBLISHING COMPANY

Box 419572, Kansas City, MO 64141

www.lillenas.com

Contents

Wonderful Peace

W. G. COOPER
Arranged by Lavawan Riley

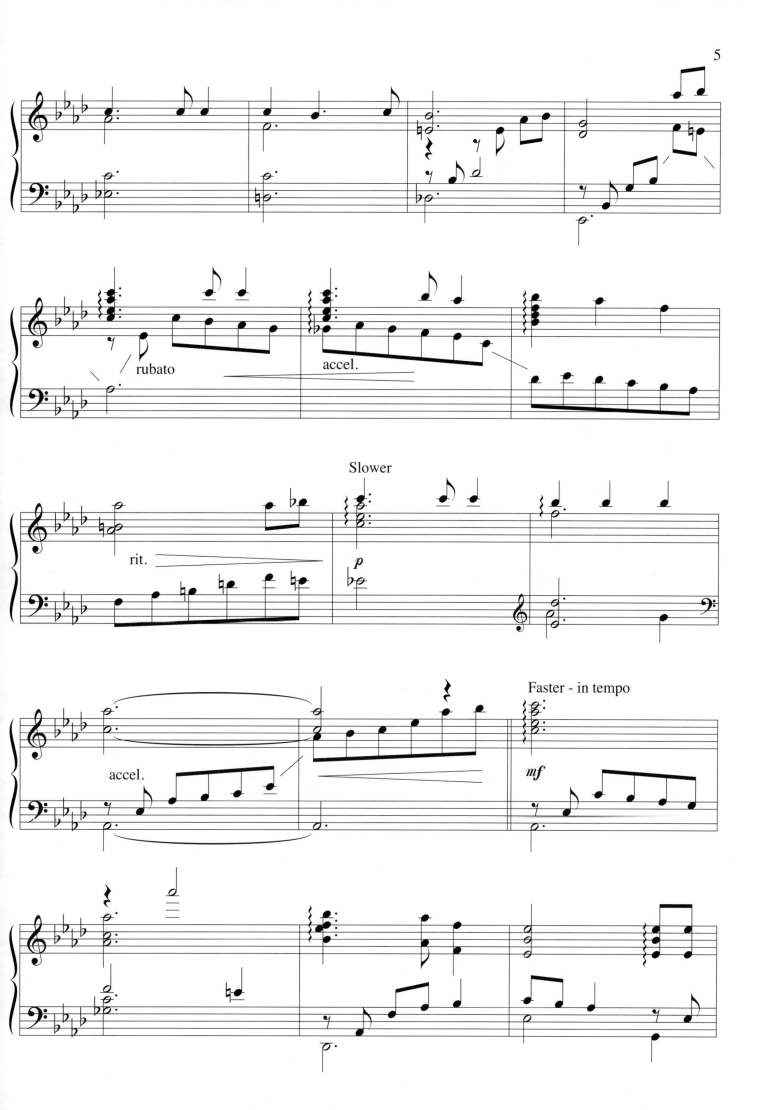

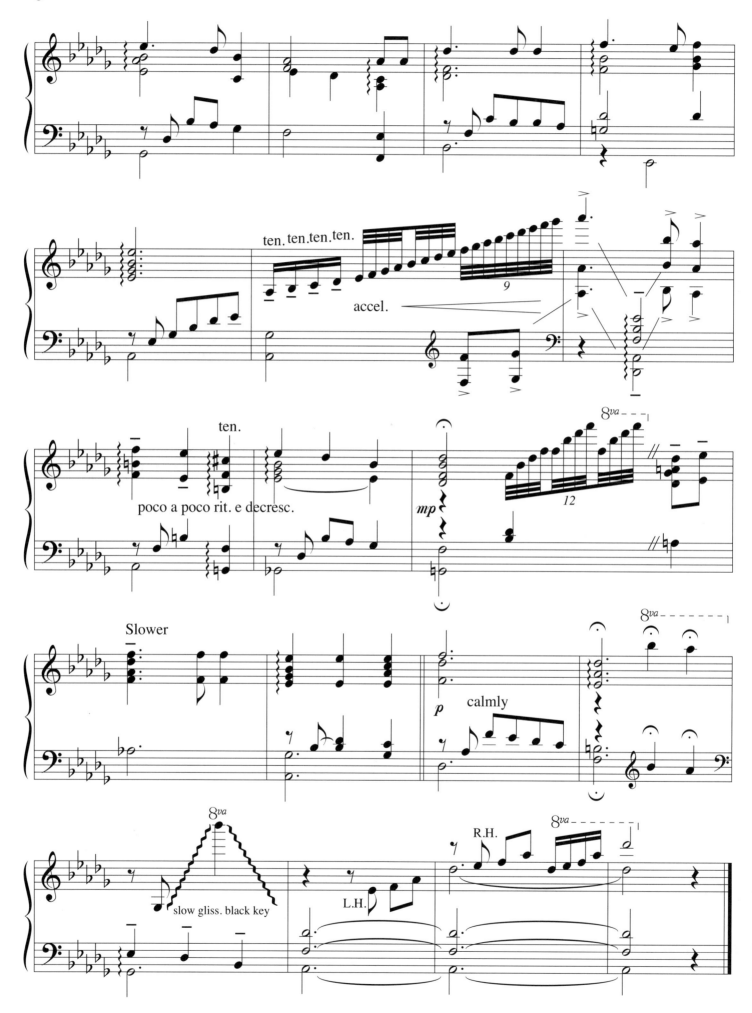

All That Thrills My Soul Is Jesus

THORO HARRIS
Arranged by Lavawan Riley

Jesus Loves Me

WILLIAM B. BRADBURY
Arranged by Lavawan Riley

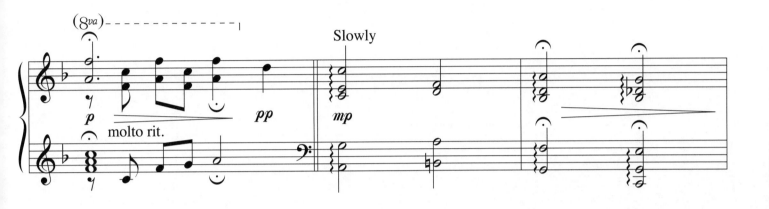

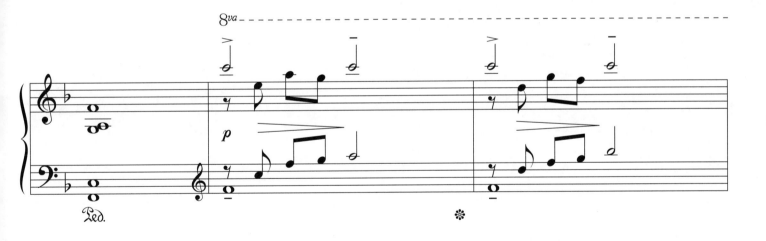

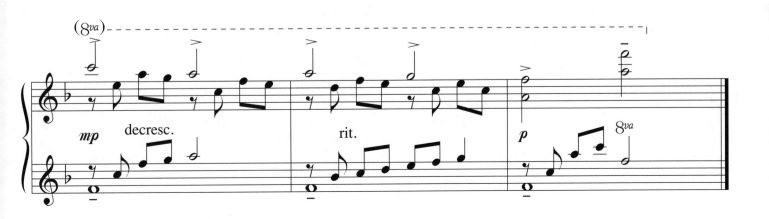

His Eye Is on the Sparrow

CHARLES H. GABRIEL
Arranged by Lavawan Riley

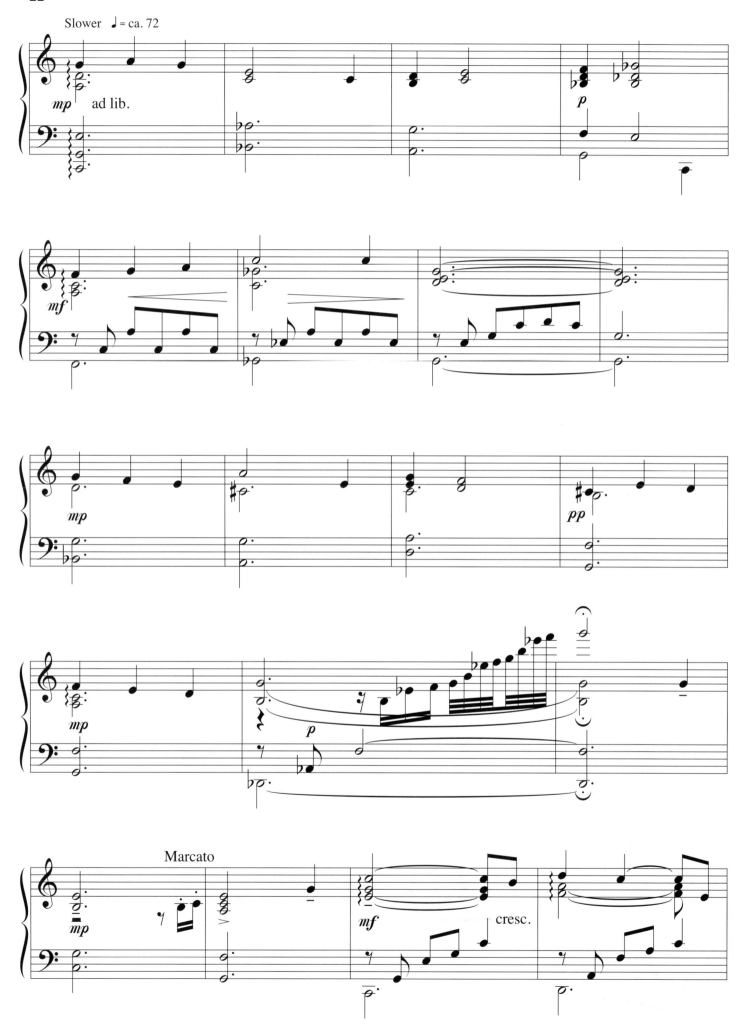

8va
Slower
mp
poco rit.
ten.
accel.
6
Faster
f
ten.
Slower
cresc.
rall.
pp

America the Beautiful

SAMUEL A. WARD
Arranged by Lavawan Riley

Near to the Heart of God

CLELAND B. McAFEE
Arranged by Lavawan Riley

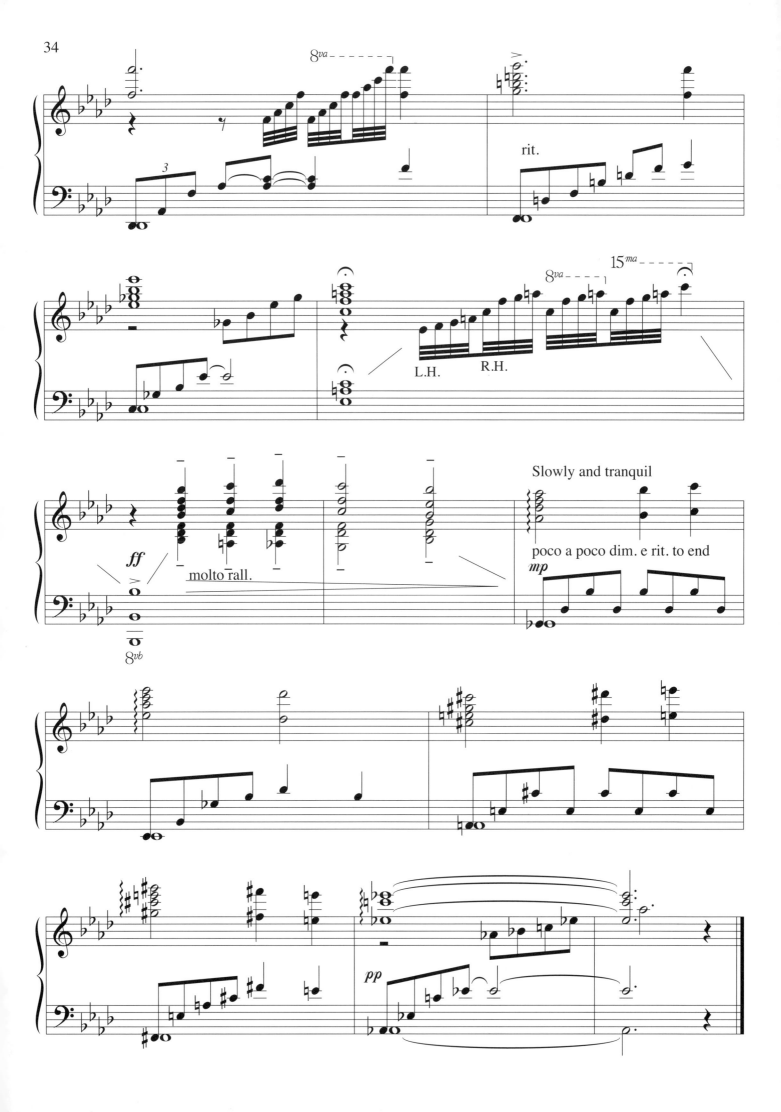

My Savior's Love

CHARLES H. GABRIEL
Arranged by Lavawan Riley

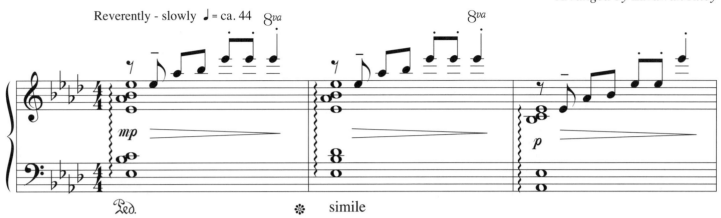

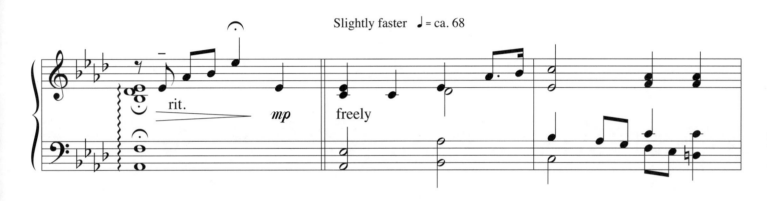

36

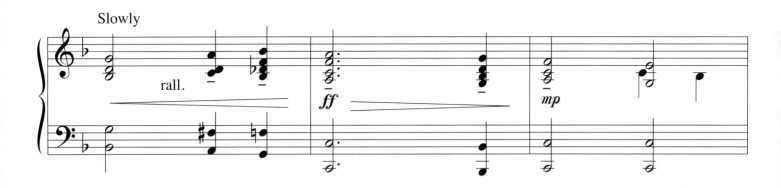

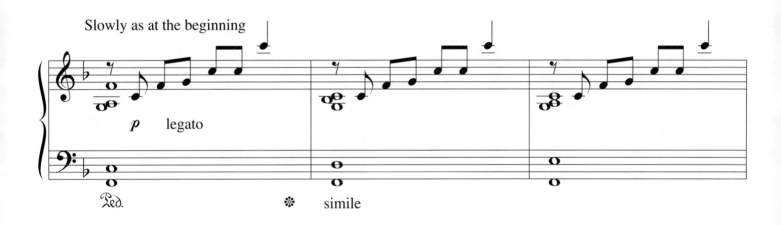

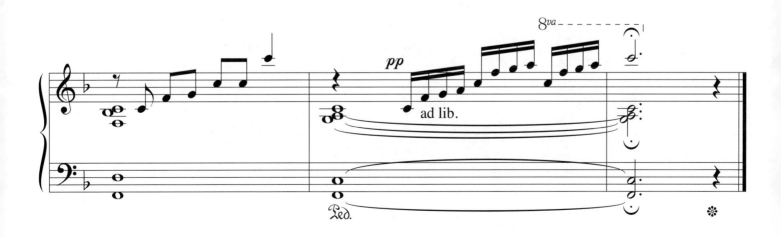

The Old Rugged Cross

GEORGE BENNARD
Arranged by Lavawan Riley

Holy, Holy, Holy! Lord God Almighty

JOHN B. DYKES
Arranged by Lavawan Riley

Slowly - as at the beginning

No One Ever Cared for Me

CHARLES F. WEIGLE
Arranged by Lavawan Riley

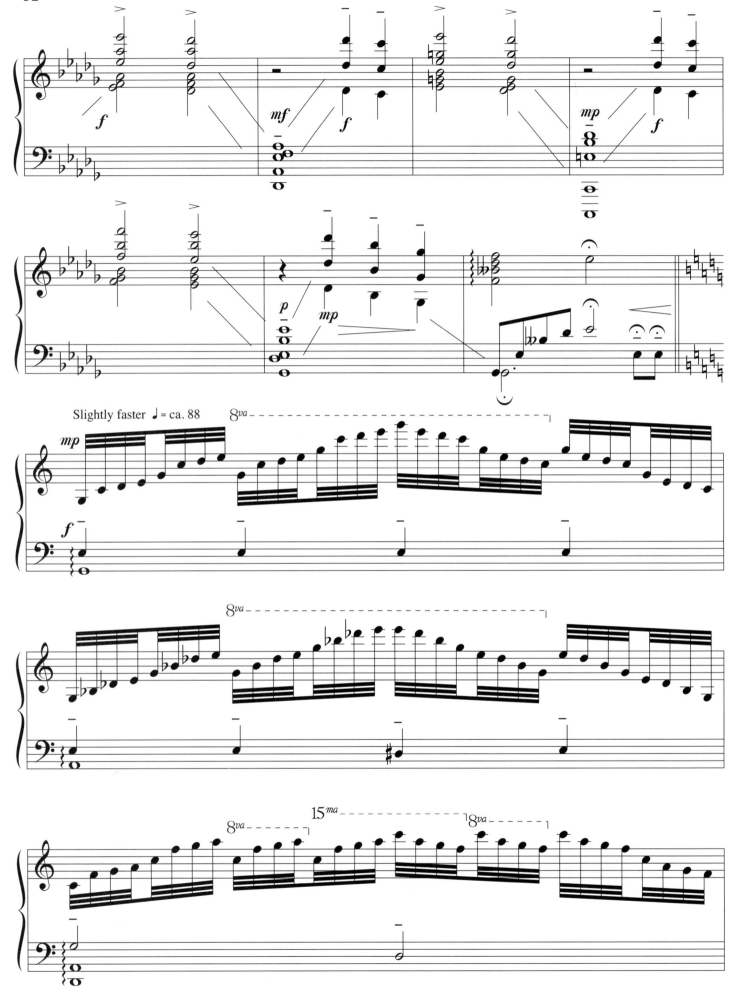

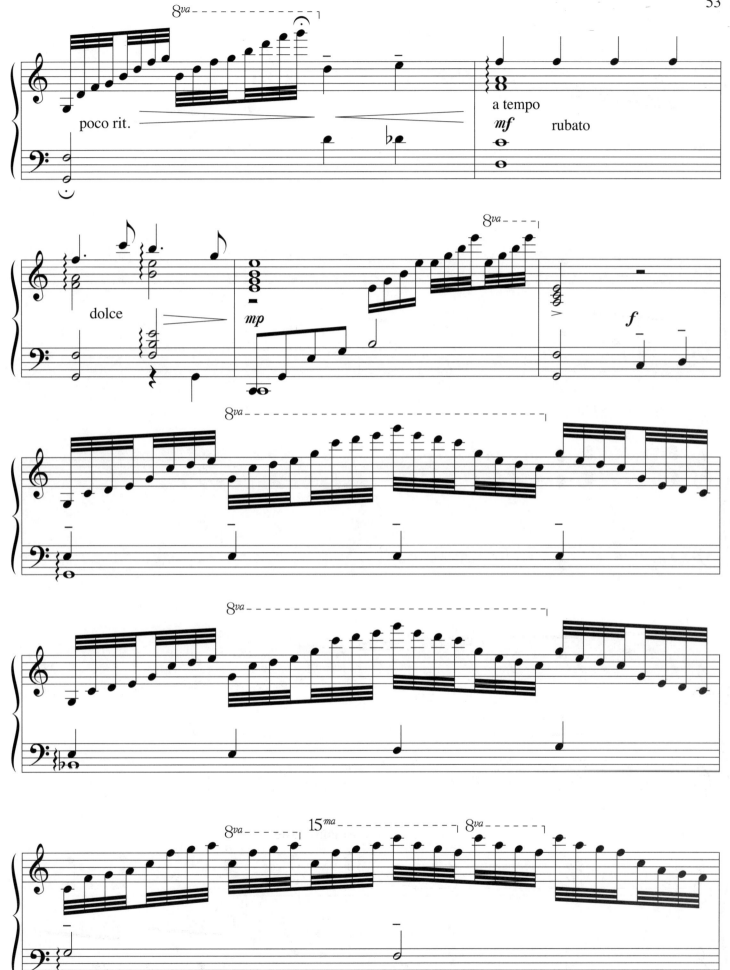

In the Garden

C. AUSTIN MILES
Arranged by Lavawan Riley

God Leads Us Along

G. A. YOUNG
Arranged by Lavawan Riley

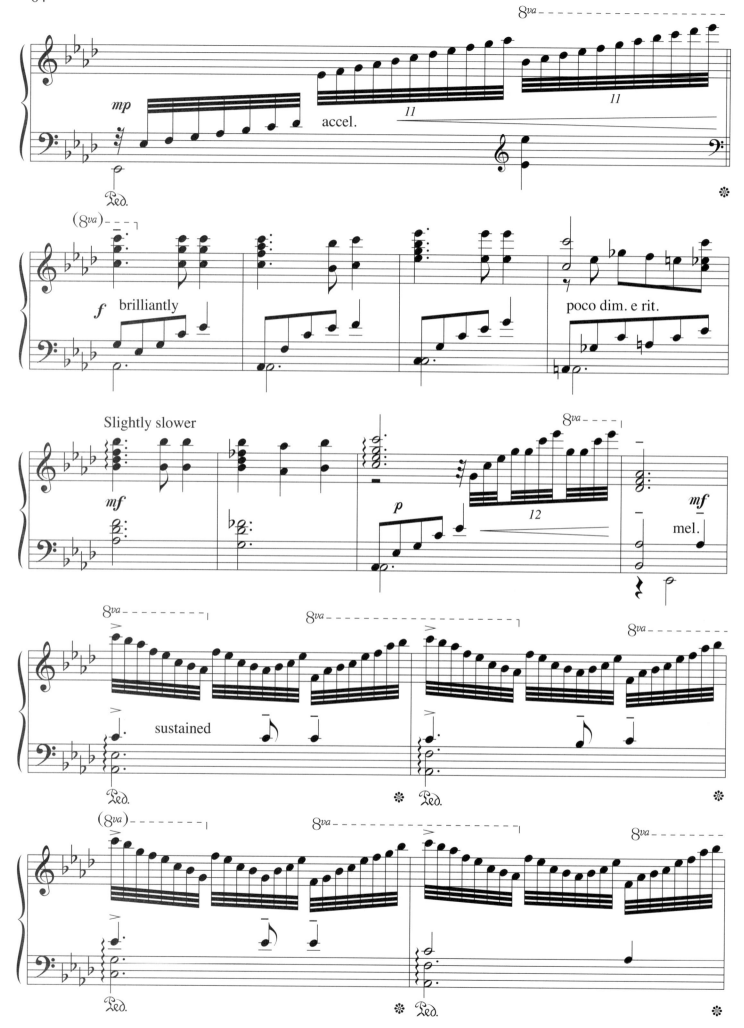

poco rit.

molto rit.

Slowly

mp

p

rall.

mf

p

pp

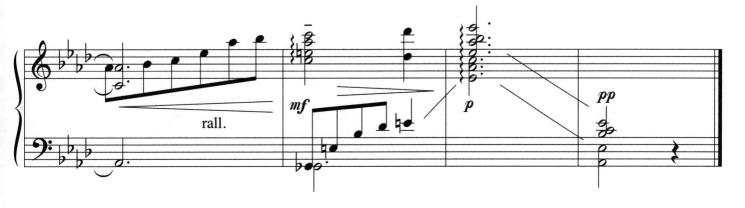